The Nathaniel Cook Book

Dedicated to my beautiful family, we are just now manifesting our destiny.
I love you all

TABLE OF CONTENTS

-BREATHING SPACE-

And now is the moment
you've all been waiting for…
At peace, willing and able, awoke
Ready to even the score.
I'm gone.
You can call me the dead man walking,
My company uses the Hush method,
That's no dead man talking
I'm on one
Yea my posture gets relaxed
when I'm feeling good
My status is verifiable in any hood.
I'm thankful for my goddesses and you should,
Fix yo face if you ain't feeling this
Bad manners.
I'll tell you later, they gone always
have something to say about you
Black man,
let me ask you a question
what's the color of the trash can?
Hey Black man?
In all seriousness, what's the color of money?

I heard money was energy,

now don't that sound funny?

Don't laugh…

Grab yo bag and hurry up and wait

Cause Nathaniel is here to stay,

move over Nate the Great.

You know why I don't care

about the opinions of others?

Because eye love my myself

You know why I don't care

about the judgment of others?

> Because I'm thankful for everyone's help.

> I'm not asking for nothing!

Listen to me when I say, I'm taking it all back.

> Meet the pirate of the Caribbean,

> cock eyed sparrow, call him Jack.

The following is an artistic self-expressed book of
poetry, intended to encourage you.

I often try to be a provocative writer. Sometimes my
content is cryptic and at other times not so much. All
in all-the following was written to let you know
someone out here loves you and wants you to be at
peace.

Be at peace with yourself

and at peace with your environment.

Be healthy and enjoy your freedom to be unique.

This is no stereotypical cookbook, but for artists, maybe it could be.

I don't care about the opinions of others because I found my native land, America, has almost always been a liar, a snake and a fake. What good is the opinion from a liar? If America was a woman, she'd be a madam, owner of a brothel masqueraded as a mistress in distress.

I wrote this introduction mainly to yell stop! I wrote these words to push citizens across the American nation (and world abroad) to live better for themselves. I want virtuous people to join hands in community, forcing corruption to be revealed and eradicated. Various institutional powers may reply with "I won't" and powerful bureaucrats may laugh or turn a "blind eye" to American children being raped, molested and trafficked. American is the wild-wild west, so people are numb to the number of deaths; until it's you that peril comes for next.

America, you are not psychopaths, you are afraid to be your true selves-but truth came to set us free from such bondage. I came to remind you to truly live your best life! If you really want to live your best life, find something worth dying for. I found it being genuinely kind. I believe being authentic is the best way to live and so I'm inviting you to do the same. I dare you to keep your word and stand for it.

Regardless of skepticism, I will speak my truth...I will give you my testimony. In fact, I wrote these poems to give you a taste of my testimony.

The Lord Most High keeps me,
delivering me from the snares of mine enemies.

By the end of this read I will ask you to make a choice: when you finish, if you are still confused as to what that choice is, then so be it. However, if these words resonate with you, it's because you have a warrior spirit inside of you, yearning to train and fight. You have a fighter inside of you and they are willing to fight for something. The question is "what could it be?" Is there anything worth dying for?

There is a war going on outside, I'm sure you knew. The war is psychological in nature, economic in stature and social in function. What does that mean to you?

Are you willing to suit up, in the full armor of God and fight for what you believe in?

Are you tired of laying down and playing nice to people that over talk you?

Are you not fed up with empty lies and deceit?

Are your bellies not hungry from the agonizing nights of famine?

Have you not been working and preparing to meet opportunities that lay before you?

Rise up celestial people and take what is yours.

All celestial people get up and embrace your now! I dare anyone that claims to speak life, try and take my crown! I dare everyone that walks this earth to a challenge…I dare you to love yourselves to the best of your ability and only then, do I dare you to judge another. Maybe you will find, it takes a lifetime to judge oneself. I dare you to be gentle with yourself and mindful of your thoughts but transparent about them as well. I dare you to live your best life!

It's a difficult task, purifying the minds and hearts of a broken people. It was the most difficult task doing it for myself. Yet, I am liberated by the thoughts of men who came before me and I will die before I allow lies to eclipse my truth. I challenge you to put 100% focus on yourself and only then, come and try to hate me for beseeching virtue. Stand fearless before every one because love, especially expressed towards enemies require serious passion.

The following compilation of abstract free-writes are filled with verses of my subjective truth. I wrote some of them from a place of frustration, while others are from the place of neutrality I refer to as balance.

I write to inspire you as a reader. I know this life is rough and harsh and cold at times and people have forsaken you beyond measure, but if you don't shake that toxicity off, then it will only get worse. I am speaking from experience and share these poems to inspire you to take your rightful place as a conqueror, a leader and an example of what light looks like in the midst of darkness. Overall, be encouraged because love sits at the foundation of these pages, hidden in between the lines, hoping you will discover more love for yourself.

THE HOUR GLASS

I woke up one day and the world was different.

Everything around me

before I went to sleep was in disarray

Almost in complete chaos.

The men were arguing with men

The women were arguing with women

The children were scattered,

and no one seemed to understand anyone.

When I awoke the next morning, things had changed.

Everyone was still present, and in their own skin

but their actions were different. Attitudes shifted,

as people were now on their best behavior

Social interaction was blanketed,

with peace during the night.

Caricatures now awake.

Order was in the midst.

Along with insincerity and fearful lies

Lives asleep though

eyes on a sandy beach

An hour glass

THE DEPARTURE

Choosing love, helped me to remember myself.

I was here all along,

I am not that big but I'm strong,

and notice,

The hocus pocus,

crack a joke Mr. Serious.

Got people shook,

the other half delirious.

They'll be alright, give em time.

Meanwhile,

Look for other words that rhyme,

Audience is curious

Ask a yes or no question, they saying sure to it…

Make your mind up,

Where are you really going with this?

To a place that's fun and safe and serious,

about fake laughing.

No fake laughing in paradise,

That's real shit – you think you can lie to kick it?

Girl stop! Boy drop,

Poem text continues on next page.

Nathaniel Cook, THE DEPARTURE, begin new stanza, Poem
text continues here:

And both of you

roll right back to where you came from,

Cause over here we don't play

Peace came today

so either bring yours or

About face

ANGRY BLACK MAN

All these cats crying and coping

Cause they grew up without a daddy

Try growing up with one in the house

And you still don't learn ish!

Eventually a boy grows up and becomes whatever he

chooses

But a man takes 100% personal responsibility

So I take responsibility for myself

in the present moment

And Lord knows I need his help so He helps me.

Most people are mad, even at Scripture

But the Bible taught me everything I needed when

people forsook me

in the book of 1st Kings

David was on his death bed…

He said to his son Solomon:

"I am about to go the way of all the earth.

Be strong, and show yourself a man,

and keep the charge of the Lord your God,

walking in his ways and keeping his statutes,

Poem text continues on next page.

---

his commandments, his rules,

and his testimonies,

as it is written in the Law of Moses, that you may

prosper in all that you do and wherever you turn, that

the Lord may establish his word."

The voice of God is one of truth but people prefer to

speak to convince.

I was one that spoke to convince, rather than speak

with a voice of conviction.

I will die the truth

I refuse to misrepresent myself

I will live for the truth

I refuse to misrepresent myself

Angry at the politics

and the way people

just perpetuate information

I'm not angry inside,

just get angry at certain things

that my senses perceive.

I am at peace,

especially when I'm at home.

I listened to my father

he said go to college, went to college,

they said read more books,

I read more books

and went to the workplace, they said

it sounds like you read too many books.

People are always going to have something

to say about you black man.

It's the way of the world,

not just in America either.

Black men were called to be judges

who can judge judges,

But black men fell afraid to stand up for truth, out of

fear of death.

I told you in my book of history:

If you're so big and bad,

then come kill me.

I'm mad at liars and snakes,

master manipulators and fakes,

Toxic black people and politicians.

And these non-profit organizations,

Poem text continues on next page.

---

claiming they love melanated youth.

Let me ask the Federal way a question,

since the city-state loves helping,

Show me one youth that's a millionaire,

Can you show me one youth

that's made over 100 thousand dollars?

Bet you can show me kids smiling in pictures

on social media.

Don't just listen to what people tell you,

listen to what they don't say,

cause Lawyers go to law school every day

to learn how to be convincing,

demonic dishonest counselors.

I'm not angry

because peace is available for everyone.

Let go of pain, let go of victim mentality,

let go of shame,

let go of toxic thoughts and let go of blame.

Hold onto peace, hold onto love,

hold onto things that are fun,

hold onto focus,

hold onto people that respect you,

hold onto ownership and hold onto purpose.

This angry black man lives at peace.

I am genuinely kind and give out love for free,

But I refuse to work for free.

I am a writer and a speaker so if you want this

black man to help you then pay me.

NO WORRIES

How does a man self-govern?

You want to be a beast out of the east

But manifested from the west,

Ego made him a giant

Might as well be from San Francisco baby,

Professional baseball maybe

Virtuous character drives haters crazy.

I know,

Only corny when I wanna

The old Urkel

And transform, whenever I wanna,

That's the color purple

What's scary about royalty?

King wake up and put yo robe on

These kids been dying out here,

like a bad song,

they choking on molasses,

Served from greedy bastards.

Scared of the best sun,

I am

The best one and done

No favorites here

Call granny My Mama Dear

You can't scare me with death, I laugh at fear

Oh snap…He Woke up

What the f-*k are they gone do

He's too cold to touch

Stay in your lane, don't give up

I told you Queen, I'm the one

Now let's go practice,

practice love until we're sick of the stuff

And don't worry,

Love will be our medicine.

PEACEFUL BLACK MAN

Let me ask you a question, angry black man?

What do you want? Do you want to feel better?

Stop everything you're doing

and focus on yourself,

Are you breathing?

More importantly, did you need anyone's help?

Realize you got the stuff,

What stuff?

You've got the stuff dreams are made of,

Magic is in the air, and you just breathed it in.

Inhale some more opportunity

through your nostrils.

Only you can get in your way

Church folk call that sin

To win, requires self-what?

Self-discipline

You are in control of your thoughts, only you

So begin to convert those dreams

you thought were gone,

Pick up your feet and prove

bitter hate is wrong.

—

24

Make your next move your best move,

You are free to choose,

Choose wrong and only you lose,

You alone, have one soul to save,

It's your own

You cannot take anyone with you

on this journey of experience,

The entire globe is your home.

Did you not realize you were safe here?

Is that why you were angry?

Be mindful sure,

but relax while you focus

On that magical breath.

THE ANGRY BLACK MAN
DICHOTOMY

DICHOTOMY VS TRICHOTOMY

The angry black man: His name is Nate, a cocky student, two kids, psychologically, emotionally, and economically unstable. Mad at the world. Makes valiant attempts to do the right thing morally until time runs out, the point of death. Nate is a rebel, often referred to as the angry black man and too aggressive for his own good. His passion is threatening, extending beyond a point of moderation. Nate is like a bully that feeds on intimidation: His mind is a cauldron, filled with images and perceptions from anything offensively imaginable. Since birth Nate has been perceived, in his nation, as public enemy number one. He is a descendant of the subjugated person; he is America's most subjugated person. His entire existence, he was conditioned to be faithful to religion, hopeful, and deliberate about positive outlooks. Since his childhood, he has been victim of deceit and political manipulation--Like many others, he is used like a commodity, paraded about like any natural medium or means to an end. He is a fed up with his current position at the bottom.

Nate struggles like a fish out of water with institutional lies and government, even at the municipal level. He is hungry for economic and societal satisfaction. Organizations and individuals offer only metaphysical solutions to his natural experience and this repulses him. Nate is rebellious in nature and now it is time to act. Regrettably, Nate has a victim mentality and is a victim of his own extreme nature. Caught in a vicious war within himself, a vicious circle of misrepresentation and denial; Nate is angry.

The problem with anger is that it often fails to promote virtue. One cannot achieve virtue using anger as a maxim nor can one promote anger to the ends within itself. For example, when maximum anger is expressed, a person becomes uncontrollable, lacking stability. Ruminate on what it means to have stability within yourself or perfect equilibrium. Balance can be promoted within itself as a maxim. It can be promoted in excess and will not falter or cause instability because balance only promotes excellence.

Nature is to be considered, when it comes to anger not meaning. Balance is evident in nature as it pertains to measurement for infinity. Both animals, limitless (in nature), and limited (in time to being extreme) equals polarizing. And both hot and cold temperatures, in which we may reference anger is lukewarm when compared to the excellence of balance.

The docile black man: his name is Nathaniel. He is well-mannered, well-spoken, attempts to dress well to impress others, he is no stranger to shame. In contrast with his angry counterpart, Nathaniel holds a fear of image, and does nothing brash to tarnish it. He is often paranoid by the thought of failure. Nathaniel feels inadequate at times, doubts himself often and afraid to commit to almost anything due to fear. He's afraid to step out of the lines of political correctness, plain and simple, even when it comes to making money.

He is not to be pitied, he is also judgmental. In due time, his tepidness is recognized by others and he remains content for whatever scraps thrown his way.

Mediocrity is the anchor to his extreme nature; he lacks the will to fight, even when necessity calls-He is threat to nothing.

Nathaniel has been a slave since birth; he was taught to always follow orders. He was beaten for disobedience-used by society, as a means to produce a particular type of end and as a result he is the product for whatever environment he lives in. Nathaniel's nature was brought about by a will that is not his own. He has grown to accept his will and considers himself as less important than others. As a result of self-effacement, he has lost almost all reasonable ability to assert himself. Nathaniel the docile black man, is malleable and impressionable. He won't cause much trouble to any system or individual for that matter, especially those looking to use his talents or personhood.

Since childhood, he has been a slave to fear, lacking confidence to stand up for his own passions. He changes his genuine personhood to alleviate any discomfort for others or the very thought of opposition.

Nathaniel is content with pessimism--He is a coon-the streets consider him a clown. Not to be trusted for lack of backbone but now the time has come for him to act.

Both characters: the angry Nate and docile Nathaniel are selfish. Both characters are slaves, taught and told how to behave, victimized and contained, generalized and categorized within a box. Consider this perspective any person limited to a box will always be just that – a state of property. Both characters: Nate and Nathaniel are deficient, lacking virtue. Both characters are limited because both characters are extreme in nature.

If you apply philosophy of virtue ethics to both the docile personhood and overly aggressive person, you will see drastic change.

Nathan is the golden mean of the two extreme natures. Neither too aggressive nor docile, Nathan maintains almost a perfect poise (perfectum statera) where his balance is impeccable. He is virtuous in nature, mindful of focus, the importance of self-care and the necessary understanding when interacting with others. For example: the angry and docile men can both be smart & look handsome but do they possess moderation? Nathan is wise not clever. He is appropriate almost all the time; too wise to be angry or docile. He is serious about self-governance, mindful of himself and others. Nathan possesses a tempered willingness to understand new experiences.

Balance is his only game, while genuine respect is his trademark. He is fallible to the extent that he is human and relatable but reliable only because of his direction. Grace and mercy are all about his life as he holds both hands open in which to receive and share from both. A blend of 'athletics & academics' became his version of artistry. His opposition are emotions like jealousy and things that are unstable. Creativity is without limits in his imagination and his prophecies aim to promote harmony. Logically in this theory: harmony is a necessary condition for balance. Virtue ethics overall can be a broad topic. Yet when anger is brought into the conversation, it seems to narrow the focus, and yet extend a trellis of what we know to be a system for ethical behavior. If anger is to be perceived as an implicit emotion to be managed, rather than bad, then what is the aim of anger?

The aim of anger is of no concern because it exists only as any other emotion exists within a person's character. If anger is to be seen as virtuous, then character should progress towards virtue, under the embodiment of morality. Virtue ethics, ideally help to make the expression an archetype, in theory. Virtue ethics are more concerned with one's character and less concerned with right acts. Yet it is critical to highlight that character building is a constant process for the way one thinks and feels. The ultimate hope is not to extirpate anger but use it against extreme forces which come to knock one off balance. Improve your character with virtue ethics until you can stand with integrity in the midst of altering factors and organic environments.

WHAT IS ART?

Hidden messages are for sinners

to extract by way of doing.

Doing is work

Faith comes by hearing

But hearing without doing means death

Are the sinners yet following?

The Saints are already there

We sinners want in

But where?

Creating something gone already

Art is gone already

Seduction

The power got me gone,

                     Already

Love is more than sex

Tag the

Artistic

Goddess

She can get it already

What is art?

                     Already

Sassy sauce,

Like spaghetti

Swag dripping,

Twice as heavy

Neck broke

Like the Levees

No Priest

Cross Chevy

Kind-of crooked

Grid locked

Like the following emblems

Are you ready?

Go peace sign Benz,

Lexus

Plexus, solar Invictus

watch us

Next up

Infinity Mazda

Lines up

Slant different

Think hard

Then answer the question.

GREY MELTDOWN

We played nice long enough,

We waited in line,

Smiled and head nodded at white society

Even forced the children

to play along with white psychology.

Listened to the elders,

when they said be quiet

Heard the critics

as they whispered above the silence.

HUSH and keep hope alive.

There will always be opportunity

for resolution.

But I have lost hope

that White will ever admit

I have lost hope

that white will ever tell the truth

I have lost hope that white people

will ever celebrate John Brown.

Who?

Wants to live in a world where white is right

Who want to live in a world
where white comprises the majority?
I no longer want to live in a world where
white survival lurks as the motivation for work, In the
midnight hour

White survival allows white lies to be right
White survival allows for hate to hide
in the cracks of cement oppression
Hard and stubborn with passive aggression
White survival may be hate
but love will push it to extinction.

MY DADDY DON'T LIKE ME

My Daddy said: I'm a better man than you

I looked over my shoulder

for who he was talking to

Confused by the echo,

No one else was in the room

Pointed to myself thinking

yea man -- time for me to leave.

He said: "I've climbed mountains

you'll never climb…

been to valley's you'll never go thru…"

I thought I was supposed to be lifted

to the heavens by your spirit?

I had to open the Bible to some passage

to get my help,

I found it in 1 Kings surprisingly enough,

David said to his son:

Be Strong & Show yourself a man.

Are you ready to G up?

If not, go ahead and die bitter and afraid.

I hated the man I saw in the mirror

when I saw you

Your ego runs thru my veins

and so I kill myself daily, to kill you.

I kill you every time I kill my ego.

I thank God for this feeling,

I thank God for freedom to be me.

Words can hurt, and provoke--and invoke

and choke--the living life out of a seed,

if you allow it.

I care if my words line up consistently,

like verbs.

If they don't,

then I have no reason speaking at all.

It's why the company's name is HUSH

Hush little baby,

My Daddy don't like me

And I really don't care

Because now I know

my Daddy didn't like his self.

TRUTH SERUM

Tell the truth shame the devil

Get to work or get a shovel

Women f-king with a nigga,

Nickname master splinter

Drain the ooze out a nigga

If u playing with the winner

Nah just playing this a rap song

Just some ignorant sh*t to rap on

Hope your math class lasts long

Unless you slaying demons, acts shown

12 minutes of passion

I'm especially taunting, when these parasites want me

All the Nazi's undercover

Think you hiding

Bitch I see u Stevie wonder

I'm the pillow over covers

Sleeping on me? what a bummer

I'm 38 hot summer

Celsius in case you're wondering

the boy is talking too much…

Speak your truth!

THIS PAGE [IS] INTENTIONALLY LEFT BLANK

GET TO KNOW MY BEST ONE

I appreciate you and feel led to pursue

you can see the hunger in my eyes,

Romance ain't hopeless

I know you knew

Know the ace bandages

get tossed for the jokers

a card scheme for you slow ducks,

with no gambit,

wounded warrior projects but can't stand it.

I will always be a soldier,

Came from a stone cold town,

my heart - ice colder,

not speaking from pain, no hate, fear or shame,

let go off all toxicity - no mind games.

I thank the Lord for my friend,

Promise we'll ride to the end,

Got my loyalty back,

fearless through thick and thin.

Others can't mimic my wins,

viciousness has no begins,

lungs filled with breath in the air,

Call me gone with the wind.

Nigga I been the trillest poet

———

No more waiting for some prophet

to start cussing, time to show it

Here's a literacy level for you:

She been had the juice

I can take any stereotype and fill it ripe

Pluck the fruit

Then ask any Queen, who got the coochy juice?

Don't rub it

Let it run down

Gangstas don't run from the town,

we run towards glory

Get to know me, get to know my story.

YOU HATE WHO

I absolutely hate the way...never-mind,

       Allow me to propose a question,

What's reasonable about bias,

based on skin color?

America has always propagated that "White is Right"

What's so reasonable about moderate progression

to a system based in radical oppression?

It doesn't matter if your eyes are chinky,

Hair is curly

Or if your body is curvy,

As long as your skin is lighter,

you are closer to righter

Do oppressors hate

when the righteous pull all-nighters?

The strength of capital

ism's

motivate bureaucrats to squeeze tighter,

work proficiently as a system.

No need to worry this eco-friendly globe.

Of circular language

A world comprised of circles,

that roll like r's off the tongue.

Circular intent was created for the flourishing one

Within the ring of competition,

I wonder if there is room for you.

If scholars hate laymen then

I hate too

THE RACE CARD AGAIN?!

And if you're not inferior

then give up your privilege...

I'll wait

I've been waiting for 29 years.

My father 56.

His father 91.

And his father 176.

Years grow old - Pain makes the heart cold

Don't worry it all adds up

I'm not making any excuse

or excuses for that matter

I'm kinda educated

But open to learn from other persons.

Celebrating love in diversity.

They do things differently in other countries,

You know they experience privileges too

Because of the color of their skin?

Maybe they know how to speak eloquently

or taught to carry themselves with confidence.

Not because they are elite,

It comes down to being illuminated.

Please don't say illuminati

in an all-white body

Society says earn your keep, while giving positions to

the eldest son,

that sat behind me in class sleep.

Apologies I meant to say Zack Morris.

He was the man in my hay day,

even with detention.

God forbid I serve that many days in detention.

Imagine the tarnished image

Maybe it was a hallway pass given

Also known as white privilege.

Now how many black males

are more qualified for a job

but are viewed as thugs because

the viewer's choice is Zack Morris-son.

Now I'm angry black man

because I don't work hard enough.

Poem text continues on next page.

Haven't done enough.

Probably don't give a fu--…sshh.

Hey Zack Morris's son,

Meet Zion my son

If you're not inferior than give up your privilege.

ANALYZE EVERYTHING

See this ain't no pimp sh*t,

No lines,

No stories neither,

This is my testimony and it burns like ether

Change my name to Nas

This will make your soul burn slow,

Daytona 500's are the place,

miserable haters go,

Vicious circles, serious man

can run laps around Ricky Bobby,

Why you want to

run laps around the shake and bake?

I'm just following after the spirit,

trying not to make any more mistakes

I hope you're keeping up

with what I'm putting down,

I speak differently

than anyone on this planet,

tell me how that sound?

Thank you Most High,

Poem text continues on next page.

Nathaniel Cook, ANALYZE EVERYTHING, begin new stanza,
Poem text continues here:

for my frustration with your calling

I told some young college graduates

there's a new James Baldwin

Help me to never let go of my conviction

or let go of my passion.

The black man is money,

Find yourself black man

Stay focused on your work

Or

Lose focus on your work,

Go ahead,

get distracted.

What -- you lazy

or tired?

You'll eventually come across another job

for a trash man,

I'm not trying to scare you….

just implore you….

ANALYZE

EVERYTHING

YOU

CAN

CONTINUE TO ANALYZE EVERYTHING

Think critically and you will focus on yourself every moment of everyday. When you desire to move in purpose, then you fight to protect your intentions. Don't let opposition grab a hold of better position. Bash the head of the Serpent, no need to speak in anguish. Love conquers hate in any language. There are principles mature women and men live by. Work on things you love to do, or you will be stuck in the viciousness of someone else's dictatorship.

Another's dictatorship will affect how you move but only when you allow them. These types of people lack vision and passion, followers lack purpose and compassion. Hold on to the words of great exemplars like Myles Munroe, rest in power: he reminds us all of the importance of conviction and commitment to success.

Living by principles, as self-governed individuals; This is what I consider freedom: to prioritize matters for oneself. Be vigilant and precautious as you enjoy yourself daily. Grace abounds for those that walk freely with genuine joy. Despite knowledge of past mistakes, search tirelessly for positive intentions. Be persistent about having fun and hold yourself 100% personally responsible for everything that you do.

Mistakes are not to be considered when one lives in the present moment. Freedom is the exhilarating opportunity of the now. Celebrate because if meanwhile is a real term, then meanwhile is all that matters! Cast away a theory of meanwhile, if you are to cherish what opportunities lay right in front of you. The opportunity to make your life better, despite opposition! You exist between life and death, so are you afraid to live better?

Whenever I use the term "meanwhile" it's because my brain has flipped a switch from process-oriented to goal oriented. A person's focus on tasks, simply for the sake of the end result, is what it means to be goal oriented. In contrast, to be process-oriented means to focus on the present moment, or to focus on the steps involved in performing more efficiently, in the midst of a goal. Long story – made short, be process oriented because the most successful people are process oriented.

Unfortunately, the goal oriented brain holds the potential to drift because it tends to focus on relaxing as the end result. Laziness has more potential to take root and sprout, as a result of being goal-oriented, because seldom does a person enjoy the present moment, if they are more interested in the endgame. This is why it is important to be process-oriented, maintaining focus on every next step. Make a conscious effort to make your next step your best step and you fight the opposition to drift.

Drifting is bad because it distracts you from the focus required for your present moment. One may ask, if drifting can ever be good? I'll let you analyze that and consider if being distracted from your purpose can ever be good.

Can losing focus ever be beneficial for your best life? Can missing the mark of precision ever be good for a craftsman? For example, consider what happens to a builder, when they get distracted from his or her work. You owe it to yourself to live your best life, by producing your best work and reaping the fruits of labor.

I found on my journey that in order to live my best life, it's best to be willing to die for what I believe in. Grace abounds for the fallibility of man, not the failures allowed by the tolerance of lazy minds. Universally is how I prefer to move, world class is just better, it's a world class groove--who's with me? Show of hands…Raise your level of consciousness because either you understand or over-stand! Listen…

MICROPHONE CHECK

All black check, Crisp cut check

Nike check, Denim vest check

burgundy check

swerving me check

I'll buy another without writing a check

fresh to death, fashion check

ambiance in my fiancée check

nosy press,

four play check

dangerous baby made check

sex game check

no hate check

negative energy gets an x check

53 grand to my ex check

still preaching facts perfect context

renaissance yes

brand names less

important but it's all over a game check

just know it's written I did it to blame a check

and you do it late chasing the same CHECK

THE 13TH TRIBE

Copy originality is the only mission

Military boots Laced up, I love civilians.

Although many lie to survive,

Pervert the code word slide,

Murderer at the door, the ones talking run and hide.

Don't think they tough just because they posted a pic

in that ride

Can't talk out of rage

This for the soldiers,

steady building like gentrification.

Institutions would rather protect discrimination

Philosophy of language,

the teacher of social implications.

Allow this for consideration,

Push against assimilation,

get accused of segregation,

simplify the degradation,

Boils down to separation or distinction,

Independence

practicing my declaration

Poem text continues on next page.

Prepare my offer of reparations

Before I threaten your agitations and manipulations.

Shout-out to the young curly, red-haired King.

Let freedom ring and of course justice will prevail

Sir L, do you want justice?

Who wants justice?! I mean-for the poor folk?

Who's willing

to take these corporations by the throat?

Not sure,

Oh you thought this was a game?!

12 tribes of Israel and bloodshed

[snap your finger once]

We are not the same!

MAMA DEAREST

Dear mama

I can't rush this, so I'm a take my time.

Thank you for everything you have been,

you are more than fine.

It was always what was inside of you

that made you so beautiful, on the outside.

Please forgive me,

allow me to slow down…

I'm not trying to flatter

the most important woman in my life.

I have not always done everything right or nice.

I pray you continue to help me,

be genuinely kind.

I pray to you because I am thankful

for your aura

and esteem you…

Most High

My trinity consists of you three times over,

no disrespect to my future wife or daughter.

Poem text continues on next page.

I love you Nana

I love you Mrs. Cookie.

I refuse to call you by your first name,

I respect your whole-being and no

we have not agreed on everything about life but

I'm thankful, you have the courage to stand up for

what you believe is right.

I wrote a poem about dad, the man I admire probably

the most in this world,

neglecting the fact that you are my mother.

My diamond…my pearl

We all know you hold the power to create,

So what's next for the southern bell?

The woman that birthed Nate the great?

You birthed Big J and Flip EZ…

my bad Nathaniel, Jonathan and Ethan.

What's next for you - beautiful mother?

Open up your heart and let me know

if there is anything else you need from me.

I cannot change the past

and all of the times I failed to show up.

Please forgive me…I have always been of you but

from God

And if I return to the dust before you,

just know I'm taking my time.

I'm not rushing anything,

especially not the love I have for you

and when you get a chance,

let the old man know I love him too.

It brought me right back to them

loud ass neighbors

That try to play ya

The inspiration huddles

See undercovers hustle

Lazy nah, hate is the obvious-

what dem folks say?

Votes say

Plus a Trillion bucks

I'm own one and now my boat say

Mrs. Cook#ONC Natalie Neal Heal social work

til I'm in the dirt.

A PAGE
FROM MY RHYME BOOK

Perceive death as an event,

Trust me that's all it is.

Your essence is your juice,

That's the best you can give.

Whoever said don't let your left know what your right

is doing,

I promise they're in a vicious circle

And struggle thru it.

We use every accomplishment

to avoid good medicine,

One sight of pain, pop a sedative,

natural selection.

We don't cope we have shalom,

Gentiles alike peace!

Make your intentions explicit,

Don't be ashamed to speak the hush method.

School teaches you don't be wrong,

or fail useless

I'd rather fail early and often,

than wrinkled and toothless.

———

What that look like?

Old wise man but his body can't do it?

Don't be stubborn

Hard heads make hard behinds soften

Learn some humility and be cupid…

~~stupid~~

Learn how to grab a bag

More than anything show more respect

Learn to master a craft.

A NEW YORK MINUTE

One moment

And this will be the trillest shit I ever wrote

How the story of cane and able

came to be my story

I barely trust my baby blood

And that goes for the sibling

So want the nigga to score

He's too concerned with dribbling

Truthfully it's hard

when desires reach outside of what's evident

And the only thing that remains

are stains of the evidence.

A murder scene from two young things,

Watch this story unfold

Of how life transitioned to death

for all parties spiraling out of control.

There were 3 parties 2 brothers

and the third a replacement

Had a bedroom but didn't pay,

so the oldest kicked him to the basement.

The baby boy was indifferent

Hated his brother,

but the hate was concealed undercover,

the surface showed tolerance he held

for his brother

Only God can judge the truth.

Although they shared features

They were opposites and 10 years distanced,

In age as well as life experience.

Joke is: they both were stubborn,

Very similar in all seriousness,

They also held grudges.

The oldest let beef go for bodybuilding chicken, the

youngest held it like a trophy

Two brothers - two switches and one alliance

But I bet you can't tell who sides with who

who's telling the truth and who's lying

Because when emotions get involved

Pride becomes opposite of small

The littlest brother grows creative

maybe 6 fix tall

Poem text continues on next page

Nathaniel Cook, A NEW YORK MINUTE, begin new stanza,
Poem text continues here:

Wondering if he'll ever learn that,

21 can't take back 20

all it took was one moment.

<u>UNDEFEATED</u>

Eye don't wanna relapse or rebound

Vices in the eyes holds the body down

Money ain't evil, you can't show me how

But-college is a bath tub seven pounds

Love on purpose or prepare to drown

Look at yourself in the mirror

Tell me what do you see?

Politics....Politricks…Politics…Politricks

City council pay attention,

City mass is my dominion.

I appeal to all the children,

and my family life is worth a few trillion

Go in at me with your mentions,

you won't get to thru to this dimension

Admit pedophilia is killing,

the world is dying, but is it willing,

Who's willing to fight?

TIME TO PUT IT IN THE AIR (PRIDEFUL TIMES)

Iron Mike Tyson said it best:

When it's your time,

It's your time!

There's nothing any man, woman or child

can do about it

What God has for you is simply for you

And when the stars align,

When you prepare yourself

with purpose-driven passion

And your work meets opportunity,

It equals

Success

When your preparation meets opportunity,

it equals

a check

Check your ego,

Kill it completely

Check depression, before it depletes you

Maintain balance

The struggle is real

The fight of your life

and the objective to kill,

Yourself

In a figurative sense.

Stay off the fence

Pick a side

Be prepared to ride

Cuz when I pull up

I'm not pulling no punches

I'm letting it go

I stay in my lane

And I mash in it, cuz God told me I'm whole

Infinite

Free from your lies

Free from disguise

Free from captivity, of the mental treachery

There's a line,

it used to scare me

and make me run and hide

Afraid to die?

Naw

Poem text continues on next page

69

too much love in my intentions

Besides Mike Tyson said it best,

When it's your time,

it's simply your time.

FAMILY CURSE

See I'm Lodie grandchild

The oldest boy of her baby…think about it.

You want to know how to get dementia?

Me neither

But misrepresent yourself long enough and work to

remember…

I bet you'll have a hard time keeping up with

the lies come year 88

Get the truth straight,

or lies will have their way with you.

Wait - just wait-wait wait!

Great God child, you trying to preach?

Who you trying to reach?

"Baby?!" she said softly "Are you alright?

Sit down and tell granny

what's the matter."

Well granny, the America that lied

and tried to seduce your mind,

Poem text continues on next page

played this thing called the game of life

with mine.

Had me all kinds of confused,

I trusted them every time,

Instead of taking personal responsibility

for how I felt inside.

Powerful pedophiles hide

behind political strategy,

And then yell: look at the big black scary

"new label!"

A real criminal rubs his hands across

the forearm of another little girl.

Another little boy just got the chills

from the holy ghost,

Not the poke from the pants of a catholic priest,

Oops I meant Spanish stepdad,

Don't go categorizing.

Seriously, these are judgmental stereotypes, really

please!

Who peed -- In your serial killer?

Those gangs granny, they respect me.

Those gangs granny, they show me love,

almost better than you've shown me…

Hey Granny…

are there any more pickled peaches

in the pantry?

Hmmm how about those cookies?

She knows I like those shortbread cookies.

Granny…psst granny! I'm all grown up now

and this world has to deal with me

Granny I've gotta speak my truth.

The same world that tried to seduce you

is scared of my truth.

They're gonna pay attention to me

right after they're done doing what they do

…watch….

Granny? Granny?!

Granny do you remember what I was going to say

?

Wait -what's going on?

FAMILY GIFT

Break the generational curse

Good luck first born

Do the generational work

Go head – it's your turn

You want to feed your family?

You best feed yourself

Cause when that moment comes,

They gone ask for your help

Drowning in divorce – no reconciliation, swallow

hard and put a hand up

Go ahead and be the black sheep,

Maybe another brave soul will put a hand up

Relax…take a breather.

There's 100 ways to skin a religious cat,

Perceive past all conditioning now,

indoctrinate that.

To all my princesses,

thinking sex is a weapon,

Some people use money

for adequate deception.

Renew your mind, ignore hate

Transform your life, make mistakes

And be honest with yourself,

Know that life is great.

This just some food for thought,

clean your plate.

Give a shout-out to single dads

kissing they kids thru pictures

And to the single mom's,

I call you bitter one's witches

Nah that's the spirit of legion

To whom-I used to pray my allegiance

Praying for peace over the man eater,

Understanding to all wife beaters

Reconciliation is the plan,

call it family construction.

I repeat, Reconciliation is the plan.

THE CALL

Finally a black man is cracking the whip

Shall we begin?

The power of love

touched me at rock bottom

Or so I thought

I was bitter, scorned and ready for blood

A janitor with a mop

I licked my chops,

Salivating

opposition strong, just stay patient.

Play with them, while your guard is up.

Trust me they'll get tired

and then erase them

They're top heavy,

really chaotic on the front end

Take haters to deeper waters,

Show 'em where sharks swim.

This yo' world,

put emphasis of obligation to remain in it,

Calling out evil,

calling out liars,

calling out fakes

Can I get a witness?

I must rely on my spirit

If I'm ever going to succeed,

at chucking deuces to medusa

Wait – let go of vengeance?!

It's down-right sinful,

I can't do it.

They killed too many of my kin folk.

Well prepare to die in your religion,

revenge misses the mark,

If you hold on to hot coals,

then you're burned from the start.

Let it go and grab a hold of your heart,

easy be gentle now

Grab a hold of peace and let go of past hurt.

Can these dry bones live?!

I'm calling you from out the dirt.

THE RESPONSE

It's convincing but manipulation

has always been a trick of the devil,

I prophesied my own death,

grace withheld the shovel.

To live is right,

To Die is pain,

To live is life,

To die in vain - run that back

To live is right,

To Die in shame is a bad perception,

To live is Christ,

To die is gain is a better direction

>   …death comes in threes

My blessings are stacked to the ceiling

Getting paid for my passion,

that's healing, through conversation,

To a nation that never wanted me paid for Nathan.

I am the color of money,

Serious won't find your tone funny

If you sit on the dollars, who gets gifted?

I will respond to your call and be your witness!

I'm a savage & hardly average

Mediocrity is cabbage

My baby mama want it at me

She playing chicken with me, where's my daddy?!

Somebody slap me, get out the past.

Admission is guilty, I admit I was slipping.

Now mama listen, pay close attention

please forgive me and make me a quilt,

I need it

A nice soft fur and them patches silk

Let me get back to uplifting,

the gavels in the kitchen

Judge cookies & cream does comedy

Art won't listen

Not really vegan pass me the chicken – Wait what?!

Shall we begin?

Finally a black man is cracking the whip.

A FEDERAL WAY

Politics are the federal way
Who likes to do things the Federal Way?
Lie and then smile
I'm no historian but most happy folk say they never liked
playing politics.
If politics have not filled your pockets,
then you're the commodity.
In the Federal Way, you are the property, not the owner.
Some say a Federal Way is built on relationships,
Nah, federal way is built on alliances,
that are toxic.
Miss me with lazy activism.
The truth shall set you free!
And first it may upset you.
While deceivers scheme
on how to execute you,
you grow in frustration.
Although today the federal way decided
to drive more sophistication,
into your psychology,
to get you to hold on and be patient
Please, show mercy to political strategists,
Tired of Mr. Anti-establishment.

Working hard
to build Wakanda,
a nation that emulates
HEAVEN
Isn't that what revolutionaries call
a world better than this land?
Let us follow the direction of BIG business, and improve
all we can
What else can we do?
We have nowhere else to go
A Triple entendre,
A fork splits Veteran road,
Today is a new day,
Endless opportunity to politicize
Can we really forsake the old Federal Way?

A NEW WORLD ORDER

Do not walk in fear,

Only chaos in relationship should

Time to get the tissue

Ah wish you would,

love yourself like only you can

You complete yourself woman of Love,

you don't need a man

You complete yourself man of God,

you don't need to get in her pants.

When a couple comes together,

it should be mutually beneficial,

Not running to ecstasy

for a feel good.

You'll understand how to feel good,

when you slow down.

Enjoy the process of healing yourself

and then find another to build with.

Your hundred percent,

plus their one hundred percent,

Adds up to no one,

having to make up a difference.

You'll just enjoy being different

God

It truly feels good!

Loving on yourself casts out all fear,

I wish you would,

join me in this laughter,

look at fear drop its head behind us.

Get behind me Satan

Enjoy the moment,

now get back to action,

passionate relaxing,

we are intentional,

even about rest

Preparation meeting opportunity

is how we live our best

No master plan,

The Most High Love laughs at that,

Remaining focused,

every step and every moment.

Be mindful not to neglect,

Reissue the subconscious

Poem text continues on next page

Nathaniel Cook, A NEW WORLD ORDER, begin new stanza,
Poem text continues here:

a new set of orders

Precepts, principles, rules, laws

whatever you'd like to call them

A life of disarray has a new world order.

BORN TO DIE

We all are in fact

I dont believe all that

I believe life is everlasting,

Everybody is born to die

We just have things to prepare for

    I believe everlasting is life or

    Sarcasms a vicious trap

I believe relationship is me and the other

I believe

something necessary created the other

I receive the possible

I believe in you

    What is competition?

      Let us run back to rules or skip thru em,

the nature of rules are to bind,

The rules of nature to bound

Be free

To bound up life,

with death

Poem text continues on next page:

Wise man present?

A wise man will not argue with fools

Don't skip thru em

Run that back

Live by principle

WHISPERS OF A LEGACY

There's more to be done,

yet my time may be up

Keep going, Continue to fight,

press on towards glory

Pay no mind to the rear view,

too often we get distracted

from those who are not in our shoes.

Walk Hard,

You have purpose.

The alternative is also present

Dual-ness in nature

Singleness in creation

Uniqueness by design

Completeness for the future,

USEFUL to all who care

The angle of what less is, may be gone tomorrow

Whispers of a legacy

THE ARRIVAL

Now that you've made it

Help another reach the same

Not too many,

We agreed to one,

remember keep it simple

Trying to do too much too soon

Or trying to do too much with too little

They are both the same.

Matter of fact just focus on the fundamentals,

Which is basically yourself

And when you focus on yourself,

you'll remember, you never needed anyone else.

POSTSCRIPT

The book is over, the following is just a rant, because the printing company said I needed at least 100 formatted pages in order to print. That being said…

When a man becomes a man, he puts childish things away and I am humbled to share that. At times, I can be an over-sharer but I am content with the following: As an over-sharer, a person becomes almost fearlessly transparent. Bruce Lee once shared his life philosophy in an interview when he said: "be water my friends". Water is transparent, if and only if the water is clean. It is my hope and my desire to be as clean as possible. In all transparency, I share my heart with you, in hopes that it would inspire you to share your heart as well.

I did not think I would live to see today. Being privileged enough to walk this earth for 34 years to date and coming from where I come from, that speaks volumes.

Be thankful for life and pray for feeling of peace that surpasses all understanding. True peace is no secret, it is the universal ability to be free with yourself and with others.

Despite being divided by petty differences, the human race is one people. We are one people and reconciliation is almost always possible. Our existence alone is proof that reconciliation is always possible. For example, the DNA in which life is built seems to hold a narrative. Life and death are one, just as the river and sea are both one. The late-great Khalil Gibran closed out his brilliant masterpiece, The Prophet, with a poetic story on death. It reads:

Then Almitra spoke, saying, we would ask now of death.

And he (the prophet) said: You would know the secret of death.

But how shall you find it unless you seek it in the heart of life?

The owl whose night-bound eyes are blind unto the day cannot unveil the mystery of light.

If you would indeed behold the spirit of death, open your heart wide unto the body of life.

For life and death are one, even as the river and sea are one.

In the depth of your hopes and desires lies your silent knowledge of the beyond;

And like seeds dreaming beneath the snow your heart dreams of spring.

Trust the dreams, for in them is hidden the gate to eternity.

Your fear of death is but trembling of the shepherd when he stands before the king

whose hand is to be laid upon him in honor.
Is the shepherd not joyful beneath his trembling,
that he shall wear the mark of the king?
 Yet is he not more mindful of his trembling?

For what is it to die but to stand naked
in the wind and to melt into the sun?
And what is it to cease breathing,
but to free the breath from its restless tides,
that it may rise and expand and seek God
unencumbered?

Only when you drink from the water
of the river of silence shall you indeed sing.
And when you have reached the mountain-top,
then you shall begin to climb.
And when the earth shall claim your limbs,
then you shall truly dance.[1]

---

[1] Gibran, Kahlil. *The Prophet*. New York: Penguin Random House, 1923.

Death can be a scary topic for many but I have found much life, peace and joy reflecting on death. In my life, reconciliation is worked through genuine acceptance of death. Live to have fun with you purpose! Everyone walking the earth is one of a kind.

If every single person on the entire globe, decided to walk boldly in their purpose, loving on themselves, and others, then this world could be a potential garden which mirrors heaven.

Every person on the face of the earth has a purpose. We were all born with a purpose. Choosing to embark on our purpose is up to us. What becomes necessary for any person to fulfill their purpose? Opportunity is the answer and yet, the opportunity lies in the inhale and exhale of the magical breath. The opportunity to truly live your best life is in the present moment, the breath.

Fear of death will only inhibit or handicap you from fulfilling your very purpose.

A Bible passage, Philippians 4:8-9 reads:

> *Whatsoever things are true, whatsoever things are honorable, whatsoever things are just, whatsoever things are pure, whatsoever things are lovely, whatsoever things are of good report; if there be any virtue, and if there be any praise, think on these things. The things which ye both learned and received and heard and saw in me, these things do: and the God of peace shall be with you.*

These words remind me that certain things like principle can be eternal. As it pertains to the notion of death: Eternal life conquers death because death cannot end anything eternal. Death in life is simply the completion of a work and the transition into something else. All-in all, death is simply an event. The biggest takeaway from this compilation should be please do not allow fear to stop you from living a life, driven by purpose and passion.

Do not allow a fear of death or completing your work, detour you from living the best life you can possibly live.

The double helix outlined in basic biology tells a beautiful story of reconciliation, regardless of almost any infraction. **Note:** The following example is a gross-oversimplification but if two antiparallel strands (opposing strands) can join together by one of the weakest bonds in the universe, then resolution is always possible. The hydrogen bond is only stronger than the dipole-dipole Van Der Waals interaction. For those of you not familiar with DNA, these are minutiae details to consider.

In a general sense, DNA is the foundation of all organic life or better yet, the development and function of living things. This is important because all people have DNA flowing throughout their veins and as long as we are breathing, there is evidence of the possibility to reconcile (all things broken).

I shall conquer every demon that lurks in my midst and I am almost certain this is possible. I look forward to reuniting with my children after a year of not seeing them. However, I also sit with gratitude, knowing that Love is faithful. Meanwhile, I am vigilant, standing ready to fight for what I believe in, because Love conquers all.

As a man I have nothing and no one but God on High to thank for my growth. I say this as a potential preface to my next book. There is a technique which explains exactly how I've conquered demons of my past.

There is an ability to maintain peace internally and externally, regardless of opposition and a genuinely kind heart proves this to be so. Hopefully, you understand why I wrote this compilation of poems, more importantly I hope you understand why someone like me decided to share this small token of my love.

Before closing, thank you for taking the time to read these poems. As mentioned in the introduction, this book was written in hopes of being good medicine in addition to being entertaining. I talk and write the way I do because in a lot of ways I am simply a rebel. In almost every aspect of life, especially when it comes to the acceptance of the majority, I can only be me. In my earlier years I was taught to live my life certain way. I was raised in the church, and became a military man, at age 17. One could argue I found it relatively simple to be docile. Now, I prefer to follow my own instincts, the gut feeling...my conscience. I prefer to march to the beat of my own drum.

Sharing these poems was a way of sharing the spiritual awakening of my conscience. Actualizing myself as a man, has proven to be the most challenging and most rewarding responsibility I have ever discovered. What did/does it mean to actualize myself? It means to affirm myself in the present moment of this actual world. Which is also to say until I cease to exist: I am here.

By no means am I claiming nor wanting to be your role model of how to behave or speak. As I mentioned earlier, I am simply sharing my truth with you. If I am advocating for anything, it's simply for you to do the same with your words. Tell the truth and shame the devil.

Self-Love is the key to eternal life

Contributions by

J'marcus Atkins
Andrew Powers
Michael Yang
Brian Murray
Elliot Flett

Acknowledgments

Thank you to my Lord and savior. To my
beautiful family: I struggle as a man to be the
best version of myself. I have fumbled my way
through failures of protecting our family unit.
I pray love redeems time for our prosperity
and peace reigns eternally.
God blessed me with you and the beautiful
support system I overlooked for way too long.
I acknowledge my daughter's mother Karen,
for being the special woman you are. I pray
we can move together in our purpose as
parents. Family is the most beautiful institution
ordained by God, let's all build it on a
foundation of truth.

Made in the USA
San Bernardino, CA
07 February 2020